LIGHTNING BOLT BOOKS™

Let's Look at Iguanas

Judith Jango-Cohen

Lerner Publications Company
Minneapolis

Lerner Publications Company
A division of Lerner Publishing Group, Inc.
241 First Avenue North
Minneapolis, MN 55401 U.S.A.

Website address: www.lernerbooks.com

Library of Congress Cataloging-in-Publication Data

Jango-Cohen, Judith.
    Let's look at iguanas / by Judith Jango-Cohen.
        p. cm. — (Lightning bolt books™—Animal close-ups)
    Includes index.
    ISBN 978-0-7613-3888-8 (lib. bdg. : alk. paper)
    1. Desert iguana—Juvenile literature. I. Title.
    QL666.L25J36 2010
    597.95'421754—dc22   2008051857

Manufactured in the United States of America
1 2 3 4 5 6 — BP — 15 14 13 12 11 10

Contents

A Scaly Reptile

Look at those claws and that bumpy skin! Is this a dinosaur?

No! This animal is an iguana. Iguanas are reptiles.

Some reptiles have short, stubby legs—like this iguana. Other reptiles, like snakes, have no legs at all.

Reptiles have scaly skin.
Scales are hard like your nails.
They help hold in water.

Hard scales protect iguanas
and other reptiles.

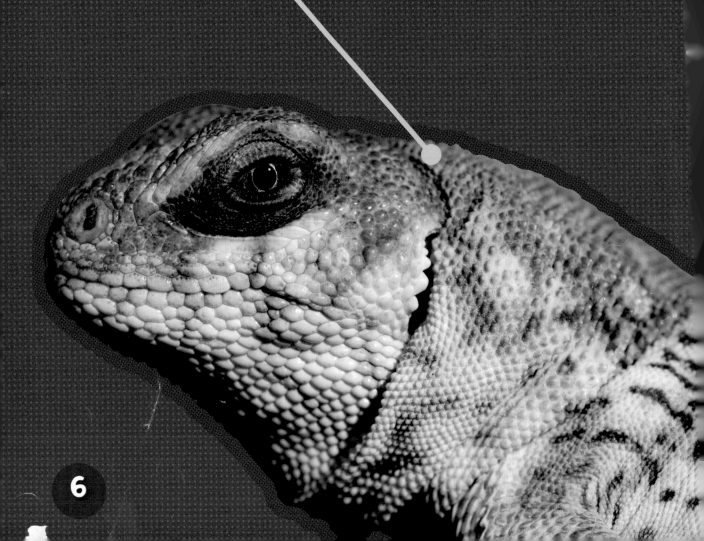

With scaly skin, reptiles can live in dry places. They can live in hot places too. Where do iguanas live?

Hot places make good homes for some iguanas.

These iguanas live near the sea. Other iguanas live in rain forests.

Desert iguanas live in the hot and dry desert.

Desert iguanas live in the deserts of the southwestern United States and northern Mexico.

Basking Iguanas

Most desert animals rest in the shade in the hot afternoon. What do desert iguanas do?

Desert iguanas bask in the sun in the hot afternoon.

Iguanas bask to stay warm. Iguanas are ectotherms. Ectotherms cannot make their own body heat. Their body heat changes to match the warmth or cold around them.

This iguana lies on a warm rock in the sun.

An iguana cools off in the shade.

Climbing Iguanas

Even a desert iguana can get too hot. Then it climbs into a shady bush to cool off.

The iguana uses its claws to climb. The claws of an iguana are sharp. They grip the bark.

An iguana's sharp claws allow it to easily hold onto branches.

An iguana finds food in the bushes.

15

Desert iguanas eat leaves, fruits, and flowers.

This iguana has a mouthful of cactus!

Iguana Territories

An iguana eats and basks in its territory.

A territory is an iguana's very own place. An iguana keeps other iguanas out of its territory.

An iguana keeps a sharp eye out for other animals in its territory.

A desert iguana can be hard to see in its territory. The iguana's skin blends in with the stones, sand, and trees.

Animals that blend in
with their background are
camouflaged.

Can you find the
camouflaged iguana
hiding here?

Iguana Predators

A camouflaged iguana can hide from predators. Predators are animals that hunt and eat other animals.

Roadrunners hunt and eat iguanas.

An iguana can fight predators with its claws.

It can also flick its tail like a whip.

An iguana may run if it does not want to fight. But what if a predator grabs the iguana by the tail?

These iguanas are on the watch for predators.

Snap! Its tail drops off, and the iguana keeps running. Soon a new tail may grow back.

Iguanas sometimes grow a new tail after their original tail breaks off.

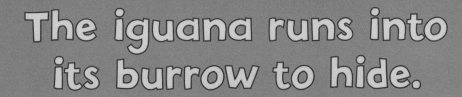

The iguana runs into
its burrow to hide.
A burrow is a hole that the
iguana digs in the sand.

Baby Iguanas

Desert iguanas lay their eggs in burrows. Then one day, the eggs hatch. What do baby iguanas look like?

These iguana eggs are safe inside a burrow.

Baby iguanas have long tails, scales, and sharp claws. They look like little dinosaurs!

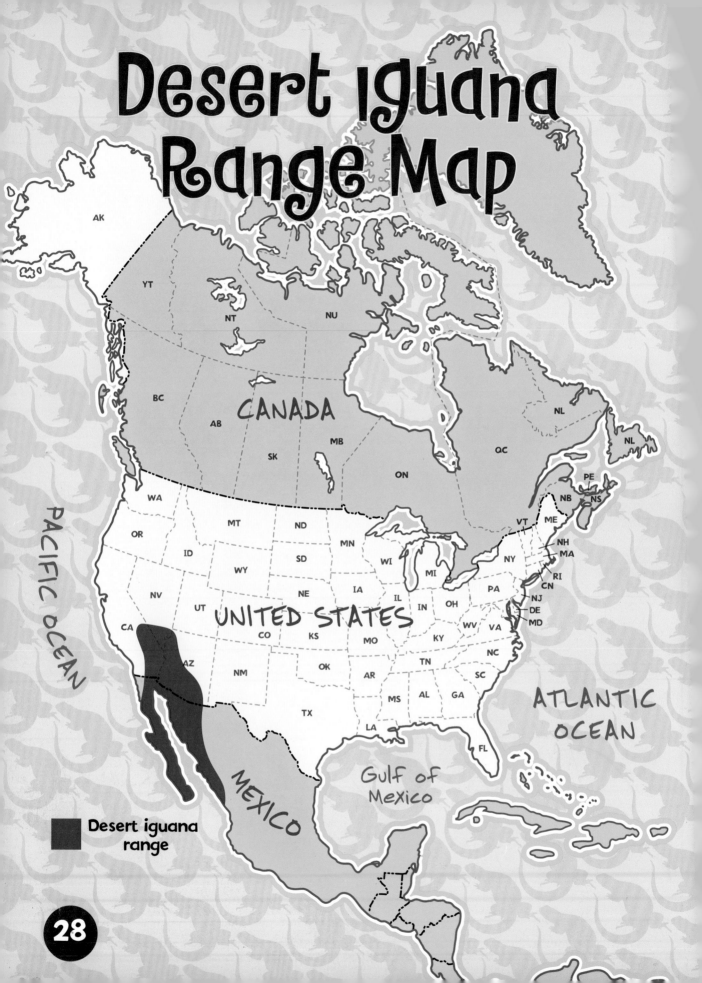

Desert Iguana Range Map

Desert iguana range

Desert Iguana Diagram

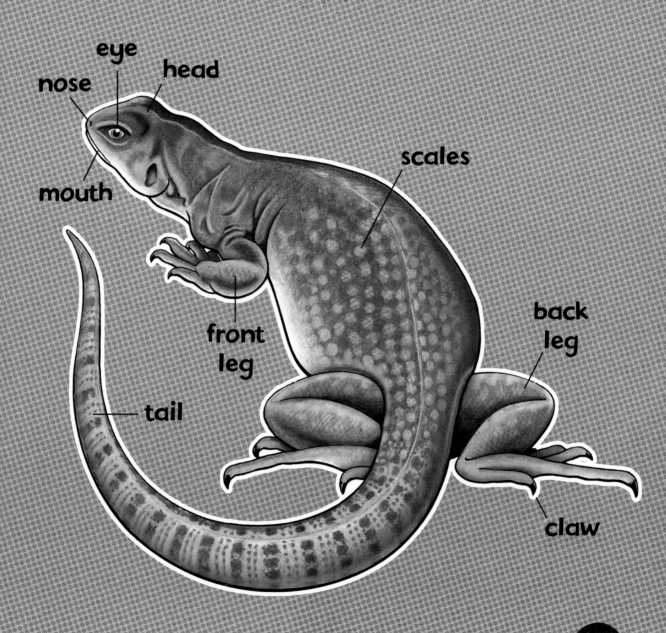

eye

nose

head

mouth

scales

front leg

back leg

tail

claw

Glossary

bask: to lie in the sun to warm the body. Iguanas must bask to stay alive.

burrow: a hole that an iguana digs in the ground. Iguanas hide and lay their eggs in burrows.

camouflage: coloring or covering that helps an animal blend in with its surroundings

desert: a dry, sandy region that gets little rain

ectotherm: an animal whose body heat changes to match the warmth or cold around it

predator: an animal that hunts and eats other animals

reptile: a crawling or creeping animal that has a backbone. Most reptiles have scaly skins and lay eggs.

scale: a flat, hard plate on an iguana's skin. Scales protect a reptile's body and hold in water.

territory: an animal's very own place. An iguana keeps other iguanas out of its territory.

Further Reading

Aronsky, Jim. *All about Lizards.* New York: Scholastic, 2004.

Buckingham, Suzanne. *Meet the Iguana.* New York: PowerKids Press, 2009.

Enchanted Learning: Iguanas
http://www.enchantedlearning.com/subjects/reptiles/lizard/Iguanaprintout.shtml

San Diego Zoo's Animal Bytes: Iguana
http://www.sandiegozoo.org/animalbytes/t-iguana.html

Stewart, Melissa. *Reptiles.* New York: Children's Press, 2001.

Index

Photo Acknowledgments

The images in this book are used with the permission of: © Joe McDonald/Visuals Unlimited, Inc., pp. 1, 25; © David Kuhn/Dwight Kuhn Photography, p. 2; © Gerald & Buff Corsi/Visuals Unlimited, Inc., pp. 4, 23; © Ted Levin/Animals Animals, p. 5; © Daniel Heuclin/NHPA/Photoshot, pp. 6, 10; © Joe McDonald, pp. 7, 11; © age fotostock/SuperStock, p. 8; © Wernher Krutein/photovault.com, p. 9; © Dan Suzio/Photo Researchers, Inc., pp. 12, 13, 15; © Stone Nature Photography/Woodfall/Photoshot, pp. 14, 27; © Photos.com/Jupiterimages Corporation, p. 16; © Zigmund Leszczynski/Animals Animals, p. 17; © John Hoffman/Bruce Coleman Inc./Photoshot, p. 18; © John Cancalosi/Alamy, p. 19; © Dan Suzio/Animals Animals, p. 20; © Maslowski/Visuals Unlimited, Inc., p. 21; © blickwinkel/Alamy, p. 22; © Tom McHugh/Photo Researchers, Inc., p. 24; Dr. Allan Muth, Boyd Deep Canyon Desert Research Center, p. 26; © Laura Westlund/Independent Picture Service, pp. 28, 29; © Steve Strickland/Visuals Unlimited, Inc., p. 31.

Front Cover: © Wernher Krutein/photovault.com (main); © Ron and Patty Thomas/Taxi/Getty Images (background).

When Do We Buy?

For each year t we determine a "cutoff point" p(t) defined as follows. If Year t value of Corpco is at least as large as cutoff point, we will purchase (if we have not already done so) Corpco during Year t; if Year t value of Corpco is less than p(t) we will not purchase Corpco during year t. The value p(t) is simply **the smallest value during year t for which the value obtained by purchasing during year t is at least as large as the value of continuing onward.** We illustrate the determination of p(3). See Figure 58.3.

Figure 58.3

	A	B	C	D	E	F	G
1	American Option						
2	to purchase						
3	Current price	$ 50.00					
4							
5	r	0.1					
6	sigma	0.4					
7	t	0.416667					
8	deltat	1					
9	u	1.491825					
10	d	0.67032					
11	a	1.105171			Purchase if		
12	p	0.529335			value in year 3		
13	q	0.470665			>=$67.13		
14		Time					
15	Stock Prices	0	1	2	3	4	5
16	0	$ 50.00	$ 74.59	$ 111.28	$ 67.13	$ 100.15	$ 149.41
17	1		$ 33.52	$ 50.00	$ 30.17	$ 45.00	$ 67.13
18	2	-	$ 22.47	$ 13.55	$ 20.22	$ 30.17
19	3	-	-	$ 6.09	$ 9.09	$ 13.55
20	4	-	-	-	$ 4.08	$ 6.09
21	5	-	-	-	-	$ 2.74
22	Purchase Price	$ 40.00	$ 41.00	$ 42.00	$ 43.00	$ 50.00	$ 70.00
23	Value if buy				$ 24.13		
24	Down Moves	0	1	2	3	4	5
25	0	$ 19.34	$ 36.76	$ 69.28	$ 24.13	$ 50.15	$ 79.41
26	1	-	$ 3.85	$ 8.00	$ -	$ -	$ -
27	2	-	-	$ -	$ -	$ -	$ -
28	3	-	-	-	$ -	$ -	$ -
29	4	-	-	-	-	$ -	$ -
30	5	-	-	-	-		$ -

Step by Step

Step 1: Enter a trial Year 3 value for Corpco in cell E16.

Step 2: In cell E23 compute the value of purchasing in Year 3 with the formula

=E16-E22.

Step 3: The following Solver Window will determine p(3):

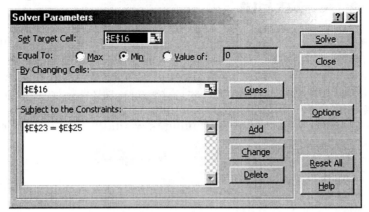

We seek the smallest Year 3 Corpco value (E16) for which it is optimal to purchase Corpco during Year 3 (it will be optimal to purchase Corpco if E23 = E25). We find p(3) = \$67.13. Thus if we have not yet purchased Corpco, we should do so during Year 3 if its value is at least \$67.13 million. In a similar fashion we find that there is **no value** for which we should purchase Corpco during Years 1 and 2. During Year 4 if we have not yet purchased Corpco we should purchase Corpco if its value is at least \$57.83.

Chapter 59: M^2- A Risk-Adjusted Measure of Portfolio Return

For many years, the investment community has searched for a measure of return on investment that adjusts for the riskiness of the investment. Nobel Prize winner Francis Modigliani and his granddaughter Leah have developed a neat risk-adjusted measure of return on investment: M^2. Here is how M^2 works. We choose a benchmark investment such as the S&P index to which we will compare other investments. Suppose we want to compare a mutual fund which has been riskier than the S&P to the S&P. We reduce the risk (and return) of the mutual fund by adding an amount cash c to our investment. The amount c is chosen to reduce the variability of the combined portfolio (mutual fund + cash) so the variability on the combined portfolio matches the variability of the benchmark. Then the risk-adjusted return of the mutual fund is simply the expected return on the combined portfolio. Conversely, if we want to compare a mutual fund which has been less risky than the S&P to the S&P we increase the risk (and return) of the mutual fund by subtracting an amount of cash c from our investment. The amount c is chosen to increase the variability of the combined portfolio (mutual fund - cash) so the variability of the combined portfolio matches the variability of the benchmark. Then the risk-adjusted return of the mutual fund is again the expected return of the combined portfolio.

Spreadsheet Implementation of M^2

We will work with quarterly data so the end of a period is one quarter (3 months from now). Let

I = (random) value in one period of $1 invested now in investment.

B = (random) value in one period of $1 invested now in benchmark.

r = risk-free rate during next period.

c = cash added (or subtracted) to investment so combined portfolio yields same risk as benchmark.

If we invest $1 in investment and $c in cash the return on our portfolio is

$$\frac{I + (1 + r)c}{1 + c} - 1 \quad (59.1)$$

Thus we wish to choose c so that

$$\mathbf{var}(\frac{I + (1 + r)c}{1 + c} - 1) = \mathbf{var}\, B$$

Once c has been chosen to make the variance of the combined portfolio equal to the variance of the benchmark, the risk-adjusted return on our investment is just the expected value of

$$\frac{I + (1 + r)c}{1 + c} - 1$$

To illustrate the computation of M^2 we will compute M^2 for three mutual funds: Income Fund, T Row Price NH, and AIM Constellation for the period 1990-1996. The mean and standard deviation of quarterly returns on these investments as well as the S and P and risk free rate is given in file *Msq.xls*. See Figure 59.1.

Figure 59.1

	B	C	D	E	F	G
107	stdev	0.0566	0.0065	0.038848	0.10584982	0.103146904
108	mean	0.02773	0.0135	0.029689	0.045232143	0.051132143
109		S and P	T-Bill	Inc Fund	T Row Price NH	Aim Constellation

Note that the Income fund is less risky than the S&P so we will subtract cash from the Income Fund. On the other hand, T Rowe Price and AIM Constellation are riskier than the S&P so we will add cash to these investments to make them less risky. We proceed as follows:

Step 1: Enter trial values for cash added or subtracted to each investment in H77:J77.

Figure 59.2

	B	C	D	E	F	G	H	I	J	K
76							Cash Inc	cash Rowe	cahs AIM	
77							-0.30692	**0.85745005**	**0.807038**	
78		S and P	T-Bill	Inc Fund	T Row Price NH	Aim Constellation	Inc fund +	Rowe+cash	Aim+cash	
79	3/30/90	-0.0381	0.0202	-0.032	-0.0046	0.0298	-0.05512	0.00684891	0.025513	
80	6/29/90	0.00523	0.0202	0.0222	0.0876	0.1157	0.023089	0.05648296	0.073046	
81	9/28/90	0.07663	0.0191	-0.0816	-0.264	-0.2624	-0.12618	-0.13333103	-0.1367	
82	12/31/90	-0.1464	0.0177	0.0679	0.1353	0.1318	0.090118	0.08102582	0.080855	
83	3/28/91	0.13135	0.0155	0.0953	0.2797	0.2768	0.130633	0.15774394	0.160107	
84	6/28/91	0.09136	0.0143	0.0136	-0.0346	-0.0091	0.013304	-0.0120415	0.001336	
85	9/30/91	0.0332	0.0137	0.0585	0.1174	0.1605	0.078319	0.06955037	0.094958	
86	12/31/91	0.01199	0.0112	0.0533	0.1023	0.1606	0.071959	0.0602301	0.093862	
87	3/31/92	0.04161	0.0101	0.0159	-0.0204	0	0.018465	-0.00631627	0.004515	
88	6/30/92	0.01507	0.0094	0.044	-0.1009	-0.0933	0.059324	-0.04998436	-0.04744	
89	9/30/92	0.02232	0.0077	0.0404	0.0529	0.0612	0.054876	0.03203968	0.037312	
90	12/31/92	-0.013	0.008	0.0151	0.1925	0.1955	0.018264	0.10730863	0.111741	
91	3/31/93	0.04801	0.0075	0.0629	-0.0264	0.0087	0.087455	-0.01077309	0.008143	
92	6/30/93	0.00321	0.0077	0.0238	-0.0642	0.0532	0.030943	-0.03102305	0.032866	
93	9/30/93	0.01804	0.0076	0.0331	0.1181	0.0738	0.044377	0.06710679	0.044251	
94	12/31/93	0.04396	0.0078	0.0141	0.0533	0.0282	0.016874	0.03231305	0.019106	
95	3/31/94	0.02946	0.0083	-0.0448	-0.0371	-0.0154	-0.06833	-0.01612379	-0.0048	
96	6/30/94	-0.0637	0.0402	0.0066	-0.063	-0.0662	-0.00826	-0.01538148	-0.0187	
97	9/30/94	0.01628	0.0116	0.0261	0.1056	0.1013	0.032535	0.06219284	0.061226	
98	12/30/94	0.03077	0.0138	-0.0118	0.0055	0.0004	-0.02313	0.00932589	0.006379	
99	3/31/95	-0.0041	0.0149	0.0716	0.0982	0.0826	0.096706	0.05974956	0.052368	
100	6/30/95	0.09415	0.0144	0.0713	0.1296	0.1413	0.096486	0.07643304	0.084638	
101	9/29/95	0.09199	0.0137	0.0621	0.1786	0.145	0.083525	0.10248713	0.08637	
102	12/29/95	0.03459	0.0134	0.0587	0.0632	-0.0426	0.078757	0.04021532	-0.01759	
103	3/29/96	0.09376	0.0127	0.0303	0.0634	0.0569	0.038085	0.04000482	0.037169	
104	6/28/96	0.02854	0.013	0.0161	0.0615	0.0525	0.017478	0.03910607	0.034854	
105	9/30/96	-0.0217	0.0132	0.029	0.0411	0.0363	0.036005	0.02821251	0.025976	
106	12/31/96	0.10207	0.0121	0.0696	-0.0041	0.0086	0.095046	0.00339694	0.010181	
107	stdev	0.0566	0.0065	0.038848	0.10584982	0.103146904	0.056596	0.05659541	0.056596	stdev
108	mean	0.02773	0.0135	0.029689	0.045232143	0.051132143	0.036843	0.03059999	0.034341	mean
109		S and P	T-Bill	Inc Fund	T Row Price NH	Aim Constellation	1.68E-16	6.428E-15	1.68E-16	
110							Inc Fund	T Row Price	Aim Constellation	
111					Target					
112					6.7642E-15					

Step 2: In H79:J106 we compute the return during each period on the cash-adjusted portfolio. To do this copy the formula

$$=((1+E79)+(H\$77)*(1+D79))/(1+H\$77)-1$$

from H79:J106. During each quarter this uses (59.1) to compute return on combined portfolio for each investment.

Step 3: In H107:J108 compute the mean and standard deviation on the combined portfolio for each mutual fund by entering in H107 the formula

$= STDEV(H79:H106)$

and in H108 enter the formula

$= AVERAGE(H79:H106).$

Then we copy these formulas from H107:H108 to J107:J108.

Step 4: We now use Solver to determine the cash amount added (or subtracted) to each mutual fund which makes the combined portfolio have the same variance (or standard deviation) as the benchmark S&P. In H109:J109 we compute the squared value of the amount by which the standard deviation of each combined portfolio differs from the standard deviation of the benchmark. To do this copy the formula

$=(H107-\$C\$107)^{\wedge}2$

from H109 to H109:J109.

In cell F112 we create a target cell for Solver which keeps track of the sum of the square of the amount by which each combined portfolio's standard deviation differs from the standard deviation of the benchmark. To do this enter in F112 the formula

$=SUM(H109:J109).$

Choosing the cash added (or subtracted) for each fund to minimize this cell will ensure that each combined portfolio has the same standard deviation as the benchmark. Our Solver window is as follows.

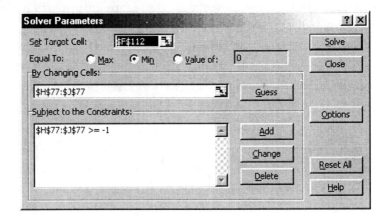

Note that we must ensure that cash "added" is at least -1.

From Figure 59.2 we find that we subtracted $0.31 from Income Fund. This "levers" a less risky fund to make it more risky. We added $0.86 to the T. Rowe Fund and added $0.81 to the AIM fund. These cash additions make these riskier funds less risky. As shown in Figure 59.3, all three combined portfolios have the same standard deviation as the S&P. All three combined portfolios have a higher mean return than the S&P. We find a quarterly risk-adjusted return of 3.7% for the Income fund, 3.1% for the T Rowe Price Fund, and 3.4% for the Aim Fund. Note that M^2 ranks the conservative Income Fund as the best of the three funds!

Figure 59.3

	C	D	E	F	G	H	I	J	K
107	0.0566	0.0065	0.038848	0.10584982	0.103146904	0.056596	0.05659541	0.056596	stdev
108	0.02773	0.0135	0.029689	0.045232143	0.051132143	0.036843	0.03059999	0.034341	mean
109	S and P	T-Bill	Inc Fund	T Row Price NH	Aim Constellation	1.68E-16	6.428E-15	1.68E-16	
110						Inc Fund	T Row Price	Aim Constellation	

Chapter 60: Maximizing Long-Term Growth-The Kelly Criteria

Suppose that at the beginning of each time period (say a month) you have n investments to which you may allocate money. Let X_0 = your initial capital and X_t = your capital at the end of period t. Then the t period growth rate is given by $\left(\dfrac{X_t}{X_0}\right)^{1/t}$. At the beginning of each month, what fraction of your money should you allocate to each investment in order to maximize the expected long-term growth of your money? Kelly (1956) solved this problem. Our discussion is based on Luenberger (1997). In order to maximize the expected long-term growth rate you should allocate your money among the n investments to maximize E(Ln (R)) where R = the one-period (random) return on your investment. If m = maximum E(Ln(R)), then the average per period rate at which your capital will grow is e^m. We now show how to use Solver to find the maximum growth rate (or **Kelly**) portfolio. Then we use @RISK to simulate the Kelly portfolio (and suboptimal portfolios) for 50 periods to show that the Kelly portfolio does indeed maximize expected long-term growth. Our example is drawn from Luenberger (1997).

Example 60.1

Each period you may invest your money in two places: Stock 1 and Stock 2. Each Stock is equally likely to double or halve our money. Returns on the two stocks are independent. What asset allocation plan maximizes expected long-term growth?

Solution

The sheet Kelly of workbook *Kelly.xls* contains a Solver solution to the problem. See Figure 60.1.

Figure 60.1

	A	B	C	D	E	F	G
1	**Volatility Pumping**		Max E(Ln(R))				
2	weights	stock 1	stock 2	Total		e^m	1.118034
3		0.5	0.5	1	=		
4	Prob	Stock 1	Stock 2	Stock 1 Value	Stock 2 Value	Growth factor (R)	Ln(R)
5	0.25	up	up	1	1	2	0.693147
6	0.25	up	down	1	0.25	1.25	0.223144
7	0.25	down	down	0.25	0.25	0.5	-0.69315
8	0.25	down	up	0.25	1	1.25	0.223144
9						E(Ln(R))	0.111572

We proceed as follows:

Step 1: In B3:C3 we enter trial values for the fraction of our money allocated each period to each asset. In D3 we add up the total fraction of our money allocated with the formula

  SUM(B3:C3).

Step 2: In A4:C8 we enter all scenarios that can occur during a period and their probabilities (each of the four scenarios has a .25 probability of occurring).

Step 3: Assuming we have $1 at the beginning of the period, in D5:E8 we compute the ending value (for each scenario) of the money placed in each investment. For each stock we compute the ending value of our capital by copying from D5 to D5:E8 the formula

  =If(B5="up",2*B$3,0.5*B$3).

This formula ensures that if Stock 1 goes up, our money invested in Stock 1 doubles; otherwise our money invested in Stock 1 is halved.

Step 4: In F5:F8 we compute the factor by which our portfolio grew in each scenario by copying from F5 to F6:F8 the formula

  =SUM(D5:E5).

Step 5: In G5:G8 we compute the logarithm of the growth factor for each scenario by copying the formula

  =LN(F5)

from G5:G8.

Step 6: In cell G9 we compute the expected value of the logarithm of the one period return with the formula

  =SUMPRODUCT(A5:A8,G5:G8).

Step 7: We now use Solver to find the asset allocation that maximizes the expected value of the logarithm of the one period return. Our Solver window is as follows:

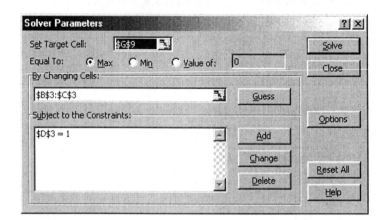

We maximize expected logarithm of one period return (G9) by changing cells B3:C3. Our changing cells must be non-negative (we assume we cannot short a stock) and add to one (D3 = 1).

From Figure 60.1 we find half our money should be allocated to each stock and m = maximum expected value of logarithm of one period return is .111572. We find e^m = 1.118. Thus the Kelly criteria suggests we can obtain a long-run growth rate of 11.8% per period by placing (at the beginning of each period) half our money in each investment. We now use simulation to verify this 11.8% growth rate.

Simulating Long-Term Growth

In the sheet simulation of file *Kelly.xls* we simulate the Kelly optimal portfolio (and several suboptimal portfolios) for 50 years. See Figure 60.2.

Figure 60.2

	A	B	C	D	E	F	G
1	%age stock 1	0.9					
2						Growth rate	1.25
3	Year	Beginning	Stock 1?	Stock 2?	Final Position		
4	1	$ 1.00	1.25	1.25	$ 1.25		
5	2	$ 1.25	1.25	1.25	$ 1.56		
6	3	$ 1.56	1.25	1.25	$ 1.95		
7	4	$ 1.95	1.25	1.25	$ 2.44		
8	5	$ 2.44	1.25	1.25	$ 3.05		
9	6	$ 3.05	1.25	1.25	$ 3.81		
10	7	$ 3.81	1.25	1.25	$ 4.77		
11	8	$ 4.77	1.25	1.25	$ 5.96		
12	9	$ 5.96	1.25	1.25	$ 7.45		
13	10	$ 7.45	1.25	1.25	$ 9.31		
14	11	$ 9.31	1.25	1.25	$ 11.64		
15	12	$ 11.64	1.25	1.25	$ 14.55		
16	13	$ 14.55	1.25	1.25	$ 18.19		
17	14	$ 18.19	1.25	1.25	$ 22.74		

Step by Step

We proceed as follows:

Step 1: In B1 we use a =RISKSimTable function to allow us to place 90%, 80%, 70%, 60%, 50%, 40%, 30%, 20%, 10%, and 0% of our money each period to Stock 1 (and the rest to Stock 2).

=RISKSimTable({0.9,0.8,0.7,0.6,0.5,0.4,0.3,0.2,0.1,0,0}).

Step 2: In B4 we enter our starting capital ($1).

Step 3: In C4:D53 we generate the (random) return on each Stock during each of the 50 periods by copying from C4 to C4:D53 the formula

=RISKDUniform({2,0.5}).

This formula makes the return on a stock during a period equally likely to be 200% or 50%. It also makes the returns during each period on the two stocks independent random variables.

Step 4: In E4 we compute our ending Year 1 position with the formula

*=$B$1*B4*C4+(1-$B$1)*B4*D4.*

This formula takes the amount invested in Stock 1 (B1*B4) and grows it by Stock 1's growth factor C4, and the amount invested in Stock 2 ((1-B1)*B4) and grows it by Stock 2's growth factor (D4).

Step 5: In cell B5 we compute period 2's beginning capital with the formula

=*E4.*

We now copy the beginning capital formula from B5 to B6:B53 and the ending capital formula from E4 to E5:E53.

Step 6: In G2 we compute the 50 year growth rate with the formula

=*(E53)^0.02.*

Step 7: We selected cell G2 as our output cell and ran 10,000 iterations of 10 simulations. The results are in Figure 60.3.

Figure 60.3

	I	J	K	L	M
16	Summary Statistics		e^m	1.118033989	
17					
18	Fraction in Stock 1	Name	Minimum	Mean	Maximum
19	0.9	Growth rate	0.7713071	1.051207	1.49334
20	0.8	Growth rate	0.8145967	1.083384	1.460428
21	0.7	Growth rate	0.8423573	1.10471	1.419048
22	0.6	Growth rate	0.8539677	1.11693	1.439228
23	0.5	Growth rate	0.8591393	1.120915	1.454944
24	0.4	Growth rate	0.8555224	1.116931	1.460204
25	0.3	Growth rate	0.8373724	1.104711	1.463715
26	0.2	Growth rate	0.7929758	1.083385	1.476475
27	0.1	Growth rate	0.7408566	1.051206	1.480781
28	0	Growth rate	0.6783022	1.004857	1.474269

As predicted by the Kelly criteria, allocating half our money each period to Stock 1 maximizes expected long-term growth. Note the surprising long-term growth rate (.4% in the simulation, 0% in theory) if all our money is allocated to a stock (Stock 2). This implies that putting all our money in either stock result in no long-term growth. So why does allocating half our money to each Stock result in nearly 12% growth? As Luenberger eloquently points out, the answer is **volatility pumping**. When a stock goes up we can invest some of the profits in the other stock. When a stock goes down, we tend to buy more "shares" of the stock. This is because we always have half our money in each stock. Essentially volatility gives use the opportunity to implement a buy low, sell high strategy.

References

Kelly, J. "A New Interpretation of Information Rate," *Bell System Technical Journal,* Volume 35, pages 917-926.

Luenberger, D. *Investment Science,* Oxford Press, 1997.

Chapter 61: @RISK and Macros-The Birthday Problem and Keno

Let's think a little about how a typical @RISK simulation works.

1) @RISK calculates values of random variables for all @RISK functions in the spreadsheet.

2) @RISK determines the value of an output cell(s) such as NPV or Profit.

3) @RISK repeats Steps 1 and 2 for the desired number of iterations.

As we will soon see, sometimes we would like the spreadsheet to perform an operation(s) (such as sorting a column of numbers) in between Steps 2 and 3. To do this we must create a **macro** that will perform the desired operations. Then we tell @RISK to run the macro "After sampling/recalculation". This will make @RISK perform the desired operations between Steps 2 and 3 of each iteration. Luckily, you need not know any programming to run simple Macros. The following example will illustrate how to link @RISK and Macros.

Example 61.1

There are 30 people in a room. Estimate the probability that 2 or more of them have the same birthday.

Solution

Using basic (but tricky!) probability, it can be shown that when 30 people are in a room, there is a 71% chance that at least two of them will have the same birthday. To estimate this probability in @RISK we will proceed as follows:

Step by Step

Step 1: Generate 30 people's birthdays using the RISKUniform function. We will assume people's birthdays can assume the values 1, 2, ..., 365.

Step 2: Create a Macro to sort these birthdays from smallest to largest.

Step 3: Once sorted, we know that two people will have the same birthday if and only if at least one pair of birthday's in consecutive rows are identical. This enables to determine if two people have the same birthday.

Step 4: Finally, we link @RISK and our Macro so that each time @RISK generates 30 birthdays, they will be sorted from smallest to largest before we check and see if there are any matches.

Here is a detailed description of how things work: (*see file Birthday.xls*)

Figure 61.1

	A	B	C	D	E	F	G
						Copied	
1	Birthdays	Match?	1		Same?	Birthdays	Birthdays
2		1				9	183
3		2			0	28	183
4		3			0	60	183
5		4			0	61	183
6		5			0	70	183
7		6			0	72	183
8		7			1	72	183
9		8			0	75	183
10		9			0	124	183
11		10			0	153	183
12		11			0	157	183
13		12			0	160	183
14		13			0	175	183
15		14			0	176	183
16		15			0	200	183
17		16			0	208	183
18		17			0	223	183
19		18			0	230	183
20		19			0	236	183
21		20			0	257	183
22		21			0	270	183
23		22			0	273	183
24		23			0	292	183
25		24			0	303	183
26		25			0	314	183
27		26			0	316	183
28		27			0	321	183
29		28			0	342	183
30		29			0	350	183
31		30			0	351	183

Step 1: In cell G2 we generate the first person's birthday with the formula

$=INT(RISKUniform(1,366))$.

This formula first generates a number equally likely to be any number between 1 and 366. Then the INT function rounds it down. Thus if RISKUniform yields a number between 1 and 2 we will see a value of 1, if RISKUniform yields a value between 2 and 3, we will see a value of 2,… if RISKUniform yields a value between 365 and 366 we will see a value of 365. This makes a value of 1,2, … 365 equally likely. Copying this formula to the Range G3:G31 generates 29 other birthdays.

Step 2: **We now use Excel's Macro Recorder to sort the birthdays.** To begin select Tools . Then select Record Macro. Then select Record NEW Macro. We will call our Macro "Macro1". Now (like a tape recorder) Excel will "record" your keystrokes so they can be played back later. When you are done with the Macro just click on the Stop Recording button. To Run a Macro just select Tools followed by Macro, followed by Run Macro. To record our Macro, perform the following steps.

1) **Edit>Copy>Paste Special Values the generated birthdays to the range F2:F31.** (If you do not do perform this step your Macro will loop forever when @RISK runs it!)

2) **Sort the range F1:F31 in ascending order(smallest birthday to largest; you could also sort descending if you like).**

3) **Click on the stop button to terminate the Macro Recorder.**

You can now run Macro 1(just select Tools followed by Macro, followed by Run Macro). You will always see a column of sorted birthdays in Column F.

Step 3: **Now we can determine if two people have the same birthday! Enter in cell E3 the formula**

> $= If(F2=F3,1,0).$

This will check if the birthdays in rows 2 and 3 are identical.

Now copy this formula to the range E3:E31. Basically, if there are any "ones" in column E, two people have the same birthday; if there are no "ones" in Column E no two people have the same birthday. This means that to see if at least two people have the same birthday, it suffices to enter in cell C1 the formula

> $= If(MAX(E3:E31)=1,1,0).$

If at least two people have the same birthday, this formula will yield a "1"; if no two people have the same birthday this formula will yield a "0". Thus the fraction of the time this cell contains a "1" is our estimate of the probability that at least two people have the same birthday.

Step 4: We now ensure that @RISK will run our Macro before each computation of cell C2. To ensure this go to simulation settings and click on the Macro tab. Check the Execute Macro box and enter the name of the Macro (Macro 1). Now check the box Macro Before (or After) sampling/recalc. If you select Macro before sampling/recalc the following occurs:

1) **The Macro is run.**

2) **Spreadsheet and output cell is recalculated.**

3) **The macro is run again, etc. until enough iterations have been completed.**

If you select Macro after sampling/worksheet recalc the following occurs:

1) **The spreadsheet is recalculated and the output cell is evaluated.**

2) **The Macro is run.**

3) **The spreadsheet is recalculated and the output cell is evaluated, until enough iterations have been run.**

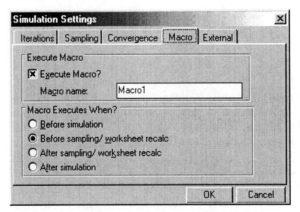

Step 5: Select cell C1 as the output cell and choose, say, 500 iterations. I obtained the following output:

Figure 61.2

	I	J	K	L	M
3					
4	Simulation Results for birthday.xls				
5					
6	Iterations= 500				
7	Simulations= 1				
8	# Input Variables= 0				
9	# Output Variables= 1				
10	Sampling Type= Latin Hypercube				
11	Runtime= 00:00:53				
12	Run on 12/31/96 at 9:16:20 AM				
13					
14	Summary Statistics				
15					
16	Cell	Name	Minimum	Mean	Maximum
17	C1	Match?	0	0.722	1

Thus we estimate that when 30 people are in the room, there is a 72.2% chance that at least two people will have the same birthday. Pretty close to the right answer of 71%!

In Chapter 63 we will learn how to use Macros to link the Solver to @RISK. Below we show how a Macro can be used to generate a random ordering a set of numbers (say 1 through 100). To accomplish this goal simply have your Macro Edit>Copy>Paste Special a set of random numbers next to the numbers 1-100 and then perform a sort. This gives each of the numbers 1-100 an equal shot at being anywhere in the list!

How to Play Keno

If you want to simulate games of chance such as blackjack, poker, and keno, a slightly different type of Macro is needed. In these games we are sampling without replacement, so a card or ball cannot be selected twice. We illustrate the basic idea by showing how @RISK can be used to play Keno.

Example 61.2

Suppose you want to simulate Keno. In Keno a container has 80 balls (numbered 1-80). You randomly pick 10 numbers between 1 and 80. The casino selects 20 balls at random. If at least 5 of your numbers match a selected ball you are a winner. What is the chance you will be a winner?

Solution

To tackle this problem you need a Macro that shuffles the balls 1-80. To do this create a column of RISKUniform(0,1). Then copy them to a column adjacent to the balls 1-80. Next sort on the copied random number column and you have "shuffled the balls". To keep track of how many of your numbers are matched we will use the Excel =DCount function. We now describe the simulation. See file *keno.xls* and Figure 61.3.

Step by Step

Step 1: In D3:D82 enter the numbers 1-80 using DATA FILL.

Step 2: In F3 enter the formula

  =RISKUniform(0,1)

and copy the formula to F4:F82.

Step 3: We are now ready to set up our Macro. Select *"Tools" " Macro Record" "New Macro."* **We used the name Macro 1.**

Step 4: We select cells F3:F82 and Edit>Copy>Paste Special Values those cells to E3:E82.

Step 5: Now select D2:E82 (make sure headings Number and RN are in D2 and E2) and choose Data Sort Ascending on column E. Then click the Stop Recording button.

Play back Macro several times and you will find that the Macro "shuffles" the numbers 1-80 in Column D. We will assume the top 20 numbers listed in column E are the balls drawn by the casino.

Step 6: We now use the =Dcount function to determine how many of our chosen balls are among the ten "selected" balls. Without loss of generality we assume we have selected numbers 1-10. In cell B2 we enter the word Number and in B3 enter <=10. Together B2 and B3 define the criteria range. In cell A6 we enter the formula

$$=DCount(D2:D22,"Number",B2:B3).$$

Essentially, the DCount function counts the number of rows in a database that satisfy desired criteria. The first argument of the DCount function defines a database (including a heading in first row). Our database range is the twenty balls drawn by the casino. The second argument defines the column of the database that is used for the calculations done by the DCount function. In this case we will use the Number column (column E). The third argument is a criteria range. Our criteria range says count the number of rows in the database for which the entry in the Number column (specified in B2) is less than or equal to 10 (this is specified in B3). This tells us how many of the balls selected by the casino match our choices of 1-10.

Step 7: On simulation settings we go the Macro tab and ensure that Macro1 is run Before (or After is ok) sampling/recalc.

We now choose cell A6 as our Output cell and ran 400 iterations. Using a Target value of 4 (see Figure 61.4) we find that there is a 93% chance of 4 or fewer of our balls being chosen. Thus we estimate our chance of winning at Keno to be 1- .93 = 7%. The actual probability of winning is 6%.

igure 61.3

	A	B	C	D	E	F
1	Keno					
2		Number		Number	RN	
3		<=10		49	0.005537	0.5
4				79	0.008234	0.5
5	Matches			69	0.034721	0.5
6		4		23	0.036898	0.5
7				6	0.039356	0.5
8	Name	Matches		54	0.045122	0.5
9	Description	Output		30	0.055607	0.5
10	Cell	A6		16	0.060072	0.5

Figure 61.4

	A	B
11	Minimum =	0
12	Maximum =	9
13	Mean =	2.483125
14	Std Deviation =	1.309471
15	Variance =	1.714715
16	Skewness =	0.327382
17	Kurtosis =	3.053038
18	Errors Calculated =	0
19	Mode =	2
20	5% Perc =	0
21	10% Perc =	1
22	15% Perc =	1
23	20% Perc =	1
24	25% Perc =	2
25	30% Perc =	2
26	35% Perc =	2
27	40% Perc =	2
28	45% Perc =	2
29	50% Perc =	2
30	55% Perc =	3
31	60% Perc =	3
32	65% Perc =	3
33	70% Perc =	3
34	75% Perc =	3
35	80% Perc =	4
36	85% Perc =	4
37	90% Perc =	4
38	95% Perc =	5
39	Filter Minimum =	
40	Filter Maximum =	
41	Type (1 or 2) =	
42	# Values Filtered =	0
43	Scenario #1 =	>75%
44	Scenario #2 =	<25%
45	Scenario #3 =	>90%
46	Target #1 (Value)=	
47	Target #1 (Perc%)=	
48	Target #2 (Value)=	4
49	Target #2 (Perc%)=	93.00%
50	7% chance of at least 5 matches	

Chapter 62: Simulating the NCAA Tournament

The file *NCAA.xls* let's you play out the NCAA tournament as many times as you want. We factor in the abilities (through the SAGARIN ratings published in *USA Today*) of each team. Extensive data analysis has indicated that teams play on average to SAGARIN ratings and perform according to a standard deviation of 7 points about that level. For example, in 1997 SAGARIN rated NC a 94 and Fairfield a 70. Thus we would model NC's play by a RISKNormal(94,7) and Fairfield by a RISKNormal(70,7) and declare the team with the higher performance the winner. Our simulation of the 1996 NCAA tournament is in file *NCAA96.xls*

To begin we label the EAST teams 1-16 in the order they are listed in bracket. Then Teams 17-32 are the SOUTHEAST, teams 33-48 the WEST and teams 49-64 the MIDWEST. It is important that we list things so that winner of 1 and 2 plays winner of 3 and 4 etc.

Step by Step

Step 1: We enter the ratings, numerical codes, and team names in rows 2-4. We name the range A3:BL4 Ratings.

	A	B	C	D
1	1	2	3	4
2	UNC	Fairfield	Ind	Col
3	1	2	3	4
4	94.4	70.3	85.3	82

	A	B	C
5	East		
6	1		2
7	94.4	1	70.3

Step 2: We model the UNC Fairfield game in A6:C7. In A7 we generate UNC's performance with the formula

$$=RISKNormal(HLOOKUP(A6,Ratings,2),7).$$

This looks up UNC's rating and generates a performance with that mean and a standard deviation of 7.

Similarly, in C7 we generate Fairfield's performance. In B7 we determine who wins the game with the formula

=If(A7>C7,A6,C6).

After "playing" the Colorado-Indiana game in E6:G7 (see Figure 62.1) we play the winners of these two games in A9:C10.

Figure 62.1

	E	F	G
6	3		4
7	85.3	3	82

We ensure that the entry in A9 is the winner of UNC-Fairfield Game and the entry in C9 is winner of Indiana-Colorado game. Then in Row 10 we "play" this game. See Figure 62.2.

Figure 62.2

	A	B	C
9	1		3
10	94.4	1	85.3

You can follow this logic down to Row 57. Here the Final Four begins! See Figure 62.3.

Figure 62.3

	A	B	C	D	E	F	G	H
57		East		West		Midwest		Mideast
58		1		17		33		49
59		94.4	17	97.9		97.4	33	93.6
60								
61								
62	Finals							
63		17		33				
64		97.9	17	97.4				
65			Kansas					

In 1997 East played West and Midwest played Mideast. Each year the final four matchups will change and you will need to adjust this part of spreadsheet. In C65 we print out the winner with the formula

=HLOOKUP(C64,A1:BI2,2).

This formula finds the Team Name corresponding to the code number of the winner. Hit the F9 key several times to see what happens.

We use cell C64 as our output cell and ran the tournament 5000 times. The teams having at least a 5% chance of winning were

- UNC: 13%

- Kansas: 26%

- Kentucky: 27%

- Duke: 8%

- Minnesota: 9%

Of course, Arizona won (we gave them a .0084 chance!). That's what makes sports great!

Remarks

Remember each year the Final Four brackets change. This will require to rearrange the rows where the East, Midwest, Mideast and West regions are located.

Chapter 63: Using the Solver with @RISK

The following situation is an example where determination of the optimal business decision requires use of the Solver and @RISK.

Example 63.1

Eli Lilly is trying to determine the optimal plant capacity levels for a flu vaccine. The vaccine is produced in Dallas and Chicago and is marketed to three customers. These customers are distributors who distribute the drug to physicians across the country. The vaccine is highly perishable, so production from previous years cannot be used to meet current demand. Transportation costs are a significant component of profits. The profit from shipping 1 case of the vaccine to a distributor is given in Table 63.1.

Table 63.1

	Customer 1	Customer 2	Customer 3
Dallas	$3.50	$3.80	$4.20
Chicago	$3.70	$3.85	$4.00

The quantity of the vaccine demanded by each customer during each of the next 6 years is random and governed by normal random variables with the means and standard deviations given in Table 63.2.

Table 63.2

	Mean	Standard Deviation
Customer 1	600	200
Customer 2	500	100
Customer 3	500	200

We assume that demands by each customer during successive years are independent, because they depend on uncontrollable events such as weather, and the strength of the flu virus.

The annual capacity level at Chicago and Dallas **must be determined now**, before we know the demand for the vaccine. The 9 combinations of annual capacity in Table 63.3 are under consideration:

Table 63.3

Plan	Dallas	Chicago
1	500	500
2	500	700
3	500	900
4	700	500
5	700	700
6	700	900
7	900	500
8	900	700
9	900	900

It costs $15.00 to build one case of annual capacity. Thus plan 1 incurs building costs of 15(500 + 500) = $15,000. The question is what capacity combination will maximize our expected profits over the next six years.

Solution   Let's focus on a single capacity plan (say Plan 1). To evaluate the average profitability of this plan we will proceed as follows:

1) Set up a solver model that will, for any given set of customer demands for the next six years, determine the profit for the next six years.

2) Set up a macro which does the following:

   • Generates random demands for each customer for each of the six years.

   • Copies these demands (with Paste Special Values) to the solver model.

   • Solves the Solver model for this set of demands.

3) Link the Macro to @RISK so that we can generate, say 100 sets of demands, and compute the six year profit for each set of demands.

4) Now follow this procedure for the other 8 capacity configurations, and determine the capacity level which maximizes expected six-year profit.

Setting up the Solver Model

Our work is in the file *Solvercapacity.xls*. See Figure 63.1. We proceed as follows:

Step by Step

Step 1: In B4:D12 we enter the nine capacity configurations (labeled as 1-9).

Step 2: In B19 we enter a "code"(1-9) to key a lookup of the capacity at each site.

Step 3: In B20 we lookup the Dallas capacity with the statement

$= VLOOKUP(B19,B4:D12,2).$

Figure 63.1

	A	B	C	D	E	F	G
1	Solver with @RISK						
2		Capacity Planning					
3			Dallas	Chicago			
4		1	500	500			
5		2	500	700			
6		3	500	900			
7		4	700	500			
8		5	700	700			
9		6	700	900			
10		7	900	500			
11		8	900	700			
12		9	900	900			
13							
14							
15	Unit Profits	Customer 1	Customer 2	Customer 3			
16	Dallas	$ 3.50	$ 3.80	$ 4.20			
17	Chicago	$ 3.70	$ 3.85	$ 4.00			
18	Unit Capacity Cost	$ 15.00					
19	cap plan	1					
20	Dallas Capacity	500					
21	Chicago Capacity	500					
25	Year	1	2	3	4	5	6
26							
27							
28	Dallas Made	500	500	500	500	500	500
29		<=	<=	<=	<=	<=	<=
30	Dallas Capacity	500	500	500	500	500	500
31	Chicago Made	500	500	500	500	500	500
32		<=	<=	<=	<=	<=	<=
33	Chicago Capacity	500	500	500	500	500	500
34	Dallas C1	0	0	0	0	0	0
35	Dallas C2	0	0	0	0	0	0
36	Dallas C3	500	500	500	500	500	500
37	Chic C1	1.77636E-15	0	0	0	0	0
38	Chic C2	496.6382633	496.6382633	496.638263	496.6383	496.6383	496.6383
39	Chic C3	3.361736739	3.361736716	3.3617367	3.3617367	3.361737	3.361737
40	C1 Sold	1.77636E-15	0	0	0	0	0
41		<=	<=	<=	<=	<=	<=
42	C1 demand	600.7873094	600.7873094	600.787309	600.7873	600.7873	600.7873
43	C2 sold	496.6382633	496.6382633	496.638263	496.6383	496.6383	496.6383
44		<=	<=	<=	<=	<=	<=
45	C2 demand	500	500	500	500	500	500
46	C3 sold	503.3617367	503.3617367	503.361737	503.3617	503.3617	503.3617
47		<=	<=	<=	<=	<=	<=
48	C3 demand	503.3617367	503.3617367	503.361737	503.3617	503.3617	503.3617
49	Operating Cost	15000	0	0	0	0	0
50							
51	Sales Profit	4025.504261	4025.504261	4025.50426	4025.504	4025.504	4025.504
52							0
53	Profit	-10974.4957	4025.504261	4025.50426	4025.504	4025.504	4025.504
54	Total Profit	9153.025562					
55							
56	C1 demand	600.7873094	600.7873094	600.787309	600.7873	600.7873	600.7873
57	C2 Demand	500	500	500	500	500	500
58	C3 Demand	503.3617367	503.3617367	503.361737	503.3617	503.3617	503.3617

Step 4: In B21 we lookup the Chicago capacity with the statement

=VLOOKUP(B19,B4:B12,3).

Step 5: We enter the unit profit contributions in the range B16:D18.

Step 6: The changing cells in our solver model will be the amount made in each plant each year that is shipped to each customer. Enter trial values for these quantities in the cell range B34:G39.

Step 7: Compare the amount made in each plant with the plant capacity. For example, for Dallas the amount made during year 1 is computed in B28 with the formula

= SUM(C34:C36),

and the Dallas plant capacity is entered in B30 with the formula

= $B$20.

Copying these formulas to Columns C-G sets us up to compare the amount shipped out of Dallas each year to the Dallas capacity.

Similarly, in B31:G31 we compute the amount produced in Chicago each year and in B33:G33 we list Chicago's capacity.

We are now set up to ensure that no plant ever ships more during a year than they can make.

Step 8: We compute the number sold to each customer during each year and compare it to the demand of each customer. For example, in B40 we compute the total amount sold to Customer 1 in Year 1 with the formula

=B34 + B37.

Copying this to the range C40:G40 computes the amount sold to Customer 1 during each year.

Similarly, in B43:G43 we compute the amount sold to Customer 2 during each year and in B46:G46 we compute the amount sold to Customer 3 during each year.

Note that trial values for each customer's demands are entered in rows 42, 45, and 48.

Step 9: Compute the total plant building cost in cell B49 with the formula

$= B18*(B20 + B21).$

Step 10: Compute the contribution to profit from each year's sales. For Year 1 the profit contribution of sales is computed in B51 with the formula

$= \$B\$16*B34 + \$B\$17*B37 + \$C\$16*B35 + \$C\$17*B38 + \$D\$16*B36 + \$D\$17*B39.$

Copying this formula to the range C51:G51 computes each year's contribution to profit.

Step 11: Total profit for each year is computed in B53:G53. For year 1 total profit

$= B51-B49.$

Copying this to C53:G53 computes profit for each year.

Step 12: Total profit is computed in cell B54 with the formula

$= SUM(B53:G53).$

We are now ready to enter the Solver model (see the Solver Window displayed below).

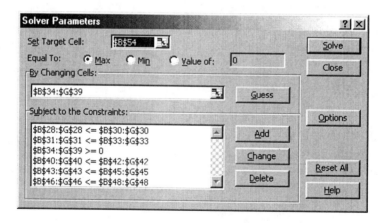

Step by Step

Step 1: Enter the amount made in each plant each year that is sent to each customer each year as changing cells (cell range $\$B\$34:\$G\$39$).

Step 2: Enter our six year profit (cell $\$B\$54$) as our Target Cell.

Step 3: From the Options box check the Assume Linear Model and Assume Non-negative options.

Step 4: Ensure that Dallas and Chicago will never ship more than their annual capacity with the constraints

$B$28:$G$28<=$B$30:$G$30 *(Dallas)*.

$B$31:$G$31<=$B$33:$G$33 *(Chicago)*.

Step 5: Ensure that each customer will never be shipped more than they want to buy during a year with the constraints

$B$40:$G$40<=$B$42:$G$42 *(Customer 1)*.

$B$43:$G$43<=$B$45:$G$45 *(Customer 2)*.

$B$46:$G$46<=$B$48:$G$48 *(Customer 3)*.

Setting up the Macro

We now set up a Macro that will

- Generate random demands for each customer for each of the six years.
- Copies these demands (with Paste Special Values) to the solver model and solves the Solver model for this set of demands.

Before setting up the Macro we generate demands for each customer for each year in the cell range B56:G58. We generate customer 1 demands for each year in B56: G56 by entering the formula

= *RISKTNormal(600,200,0,1600)*.

in B56, and copying the formula to Column G, we generate Customer 2 demands by entering in cell B57 the formula

=*RISKTNormal(500,100,0,1000)*.

and copying the formula across to Column G.

The =RISKTNormal function generates a random variable whose value is truncated at a lower and upper value. For example,

$$=RISKTNormal(10,2,9,11)$$

generates a normal random variable with mean 10 and standard deviation 2. If the random variable assumes a value between 9 (the lower truncation value) and 11 (the upper truncation value) that value is retained. Otherwise, another value if generated. The truncation values must be within 5 standard deviations of the mean.

We generate Customer 3 demands in B58 with the formula

$$=RISKTNormal(500,200,0,1500).$$

We now set up the desired Macro.

Step by Step

Step 1: Hit "Tools" "Record Macro" "Record New Macro". The Macro recorder is now on. Our macro is named Risksolver.

Step 2: Next Edit>Copy>Paste Special Values the customer demands in rows 56-58 to rows 42, 45, and 48 respectively.

Step 3: Run the Solver. This determines a profit-maximizing pattern of sales for the random demands currently in rows 42, 45, and 48.

Step 4: Click on the Stop Recording Button.

The Macro will not know to call the solver unless you go the Module sheet and click on Tools References and check the Solver.

For our Macro to work with @RISK we need to change the last line of the Macro (the line before End Sub) from Solversolve to

$$Solversolve(TRUE).$$

This ensures that when we run the Macro we will not have to hit return to enter the solution found by the Solver. The code created by the Macro Recorder follows:

Macro to Integrate Solver and @RISK

```
Sub risksolver()
'
' risksolver Macro
' Macro recorded 4/21/98 by School of Business
'
'
    ActiveWindow.SmallScroll Down:=15
    Range("B56:G56").Select
    Selection.Copy
    ActiveWindow.SmallScroll Down:=-13
    Range("B42:G42").Select
    Selection.PasteSpecial Paste:=xlValues, Operation:=xlNone, SkipBlanks:= _
        False, Transpose:=False
    ActiveWindow.SmallScroll Down:=16
    Range("B57:G57").Select
    Application.CutCopyMode = False
    Selection.Copy
    ActiveWindow.SmallScroll Down:=-9
    Range("B45").Select
    Selection.PasteSpecial Paste:=xlValues, Operation:=xlNone, SkipBlanks:= _
        False, Transpose:=False
    ActiveWindow.SmallScroll Down:=7
    Range("B58:G58").Select
    Application.CutCopyMode = False
    Selection.Copy
    Range("B48").Select
    Selection.PasteSpecial Paste:=xlValues, Operation:=xlNone, SkipBlanks:= _
        False, Transpose:=False
    SolverOk SetCell:="$B$54", MaxMinVal:=1, ValueOf:="0", ByChange:="$B$34:$G$39"
    SolverSolve (True)
End Sub
```

Running the Macro with @RISK

We now go to the Simulations Settings dialog box of @RISK and

1) Check Execute Macro.

2) Enter the Macro name (Risksolver).

3) Check Before sampling/worksheet recalc (after sampling/worksheet recalc is also ok).

4) Choose cell B54 and B34:G39 as output cells.

5) Run @RISK!

	A	B	C	D	E	F
242						
243		**Simulation 7: Dallas = 900 Chicago = 500**				
244		Cell	Name	Minimum	Mean	Maximum
245		B54	Total Profit / Customer 1	7444.616	10962.31	12408.43
246		B34	Dallas C1 / Customer 1	-0.000001	26.68883	254.0997
247		C34	Dallas C1 / Customer 2	0	9.657206	193.6636
248		D34	Dallas C1 / Customer 3	-0.000001	31.10437	315.4727
249		E34	Dallas C1	-0.000001	20.16756	288.9203
250		F34	Dallas C1	0	27.75702	340.7159
251		G34	Dallas C1	0	28.61729	341.7023
252		B35	Dallas C2 / Customer 1	0	328.4389	629.4983
253		C35	Dallas C2 / Customer 2	0	326.2484	607.2066
254		D35	Dallas C2 / Customer 3	0	328.5261	619.8184
255		E35	Dallas C2	0	328.5309	591.8247
256		F35	Dallas C2	0	320.1045	560.4594
257		G35	Dallas C2	0	319.6631	581.8772

Our results are in the sheet Output. After running a simulation for each of the 9 proposed capacity combinations, it appears that expected profit is maximized by the combination having a capacity level of 900 at Dallas and 500 at Chicago!

@RISK Crib Sheet

@RISK Icons

Once you are familiar with the function of the @RISK icons, you will find @RISK easy to learn. Here is a description of the icons.

Opening @RISK Simulation

This icon allows you to open up a saved @RISK simulation. I do not recommend saving simulations. Instead, I paste results into spreadsheet.

Saving @RISK Simulation

This icon allows you to save an @RISK simulation including data and simulation settings.

Simulation Settings

This icon allows you to control the settings for the simulation. Clicking on this icon activates the following dialog box:

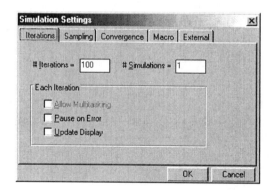

Here is what each of the tabs can do for you.

Iterations Tab

Here is an explanation of the various options associated with the Iterations Tab.

#Iterations #Iterations is how many times you want @RISK to recalculate the spreadsheet. For example, choosing 100 iterations ensures that 100 values of your output cells will be tabulated.

#Simulations Leave this at 1 unless you have a *=RISKSimTable* function in spreadsheet. In this case choose #Simulations to equal number of values in simtable. For example, if we have formula *=RISKSimTable* ({100,150,200,250,300}) in cell A1set #Simulations to 5. The first simulation will place 100 in A1, the second simulation will place 150 in A1 ... and the fifth simulation will place 300 in A1. #Iterations will be run for each simulation.

Allow Multitasking In Windows 3.1 this allows your computer to multitask, or work on other programs while @RISK is running. With Windows 95 Allow Multitasking has no effect.

Pause on Error Checking this box causes @RISK to pause if an error occurs in any cell during the simulation, @RISK will highlight the cells where the error occurs.

Update Display Checking this box causes @RISK to show the results of each iteration on the screen. This is nice, but it slows things down.

Sampling Tab

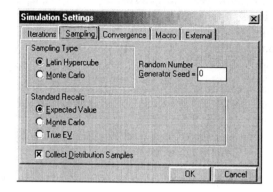

Here is an explanation of the Sampling tab options.

Sampling Type

While a little slower, Latin Hypercube sampling is much more accurate than Monte Carlo sampling. To illustrate Latin Hypercube guarantees for a given cell that 5% of observations will come from the bottom 5th percentile of actual random variable, 5% will come from top 5th percentile of actual random variable, etc. If we choose Monte Carlo sampling, then it is possible, for example, that 8% of our observations may come from bottom 5% of actual distribution, when in reality only 5% of observations should come from bottom 5% of actual distribution. When simulating financial derivatives, it is crucial to use Latin Hypercube.

Standard Recalc

If you choose Expected Value you obtain the Expected Value of the random variable unless random variable is discrete. Then you obtain the possible value of random variable that is closest to the random variable's expected value. For instance, for a statement

=RISKDiscrete({1,2,},{.6,.4})

the expected value is 1(.6) + 2(.4) = 1.4, so Expected Value enters a 1.

If you choose the Monte Carlo option, then **when you hit F9 all your random cells will recalculate. This makes it much easier to understand and debug your spreadsheet.** Thus with Monte Carlo selected

=RISKDiscrete({1,2,},{.6,.4})

will return a "1" 60% of the time and a "2" 40% of the time.

If you choose the TRUE EV option, then the actual expected value of the random variable will be returned. Thus

=RISKDiscrete({1,2,},{.6,.4})

will yield a 1.4.

**Collecting
Distribution
Samples**
Check this box if you want to get Tornado Graphs, a Scenario Analysis, or Extract Data. Also check this box if you want statistics on cells generated by @RISK functions. You can always check this box if you like, but if you do not need it and you have many @RISK functions in your spreadsheet checking the box will slow down your spreadsheet.

**Random
Number
Generator
Seed**
When the seed is set to 0, each time you run a simulation you will obtain different results. Other possible seed values are integers between 1 and 32,767. Whenever a non-zero seed is chosen the same values for the input cells and output cells will occur. For example, if we choose a seed value of, say, 10, then each time we run the simulation we will obtain **exactly the same results**.

Convergence Tab

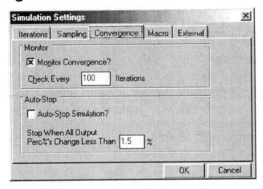

**Monitor
Convergence**
If you check Monitor Convergence box and choose, say 100 iterations, then for every 100 iterations @RISK monitors the percentage change in the mean, standard deviation, and percentiles for all output cells. After many (we do not know how many!) iterations these percentage changes should be near 0. This means we have run enough iterations to zero in on the mean, standard deviation, and percentiles of our output cells.

We have learned how to use confidence intervals to determine how many iterations to run in a simulation. Alternatively, we can check the Autostop Simulation option and choose a stopping percentage (default is 1.5%). Then @RISK runs enough iterations until over the last 100 iterations the mean, standard deviation, and percentiles of all output cells change by 1.5% or less. This can **be a lot of iterations!** For this reason, I prefer to choose the number of iterations myself by setting

$$\frac{2s}{\sqrt{n}}$$

equal to the desired level of accuracy for the output cell's mean. Here

s = *standard deviation of output cell for a trial simulation (say 400 iterations).*

@RISK Icons

For example, if a trial simulation yields s = 100 and I want to be 95% sure that I am estimating the population mean within 10 I need

$$\frac{2(100)}{\sqrt{n}} = 10$$

or n = 400.

As soon as the Autostop criteria (if selected) is satisfied or all iterations have been run (if Autostop is not selected) the frowning face will change to a smiling face.

Macro Tab

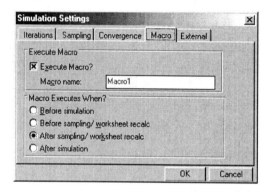

The Macro Tab enables @RISK to run a Macro before or after each iteration of a simulation. For example, the above window will run Macro 1 after evaluating each output cell. The sequence of events would be:

1) *Compute @RISK functions and calculate output cells*

2) *Run Macro1*

3) *Compute @RISK functions and calculate output cells, etc.*

Select output cells

This icon enables you to select an output cell(s) for which @RISK will create statistics. Simply select a range of cells and click on the icon to select the range as output cells. You may select as many ranges as you desire.

List input and output cells

This icon lists all output cells. Also listed are cells containing @RISK functions. These are called input cells. From this list you can change names of output cells or delete output cells.

Run Simulation

This icon starts the simulation. The status of the simulation is shown in the lower left-hand corner of your screen. Hitting the Escape key allows you to terminate the simulation.

Show Results

This icon allows you to see results. There are two windows:

Summary Results Window containing Minimum, Mean, and Maximum for all input and output cells.

Simulation Statistics containing more detailed statistics.

Clicking the Hide icon will send you back to your worksheet.

To paste your Statistics into your worksheet simply select a window and Edit>Copy>Paste it into your worksheet.

Graphing

From the Summary Window you can click on the Graph icon at top of screen to graph the results of iterations for any input cell. Right clicking on a graph brings up the following dialog box that allows you to change the type of graph. In Office 97 you should save your graph as a Bitmap (.bmp suffix) file if you want to paste the graph into Word or Excel.

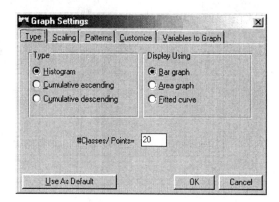

A **histogram** gives the fraction of iterations assuming different values. The following histogram was generated for a cell containing the formula

   =RISKNormal(100,15).

Histogram

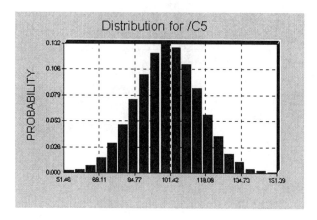

The above histogram indicates the input cell was bell-shaped and most common values of the input cell were around 100.

Cumulative ascending

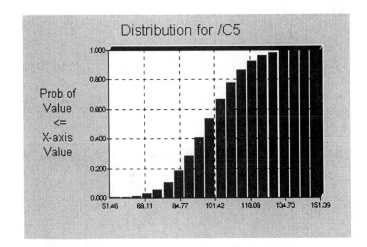

For a cumulative ascending graph the y-axis gives the fraction of iterations yielding a value <= the value on the x-axis axis. Thus about 50% of all iterations yielded a value <=100.

For a **cumulative descending graph** the y-axis gives the fraction of iterations yielding a value >= the value on the x-axis.

Cumulative Descending Graph

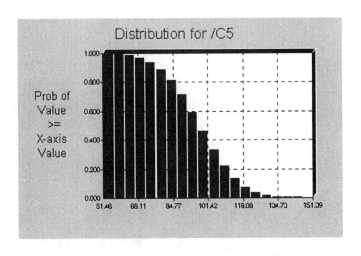

Thus about 84% of time this input cell exceeded 85.

An area graph replaces bars with smooth areas. A fitted curve smooths out the variation in bar heights before creating an area graph.

Targets

At the bottom of simulation statistics window is a Target option. You may enter a value or percentile and @RISK fills in the one you left out. For

=RISKNormal(100,15)

we obtained the following results:

Target #1 (Value)=	85
Target #1 (Perc%)=	15.87%
Target #2 (Value)=	130
Target #2 (Perc%)=	97.75%
Target #3 (Value)=	114.9159
Target #3 (Perc%)=	84%

We entered Target#1(Value) of 85, and @RISK reported that the cell was <=85 15.87% of time.

We entered Target#2(Value) of 130, and @RISK reported that the cell was <=130 97.75% of time.

We entered Target#3(Perc%) of 84%, and @RISK reported that 84% of time the cell was <=114.92.

Extracting Data

Sometimes you may want to see the values of =RISK functions and output cells that @RISK created on the iterations run. If you want to do this check Collect Distribution Samples under Simulation Settings and then click on Data in the Results window. You can then Edit>Copy>Paste your data to your spreadsheet and subject it to further analysis.

Sensitivity

If you want a Tornado Graph, click on Sensitivity in the Results window. This also requires that you check Collect Distribution Samples. You may choose either a Correlation or Regression Graph. Tornado graphs let you know which input cells have the largest influence on your output cell(s). See Chapter 28 for a discussion of Tornado graphs.

Scenario

Click on Scenario to create a Scenario analysis. A Scenario Analysis lets you create a Scenario (e.g. Top 10% of all NPV's, Bottom 25% of all NPV's) and determine which input cells tend to assume atypical values when the given scenario occurs. See Chapter 28 for a discussion of Scenario Analysis.

Section II-@RISK Functions

We now illustrate some of the most useful @RISK functions.

RISKDiscrete Function

This generates a discrete random variable that takes on a finite number of values with known probabilities. First you enter the possible values of the random variable and then the probability for each value. Thus =*RISKDiscrete({1,2,3,4},{.3,.2,.4,.1})* would generate a 1 30% of time, 2 20% of time, a 3 40% of time and a 4 10% of time.

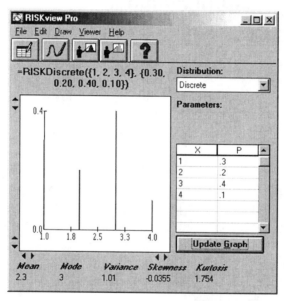

If the values and probabilities were entered in A2:B5 we could have entered this random variable with formula

=*RISKDiscrete(A2:A5, B2:B5)*.

RISKSimTable Function

Suppose we enter

= *RISKSimTable({100,150,200,250,300})*

in a cell, say A5, and number of iterations is 100. If we change number of Simulations to 5, then on first simulation 100 iterations are run with 100 in cell A5. Then on second simulation 100 iterations are run with 150 in cell A5. Finally on 5th simulation 100 iterations are run with 300 in cell A5. If the five arguments for the =RISKSimTable function were in B1:B5 we could have also entered the =RISKSimTable function as

=*RISKSimTable(B1:B5).*

RISKDUniform Function

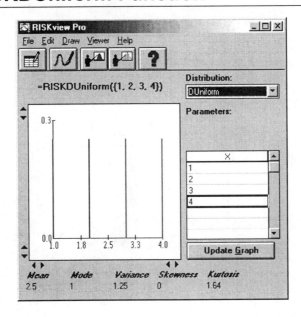

Use RISKDUniform when a random variable assumes several equally likely values.

Thus

= *RISKDUniform ({1,2,3,4})*

is equally likely to generate a 1, 2, 3, or 4. If 1, 2, 3, 4 were entered in A1:A4 then we could have entered

= *RISKDUniform (A1:A4).*

Binomial Distribution

Use =RISKBinomial when you have repeated independent trials each having the same probability of success. For example if there are 5 competitors who might enter an industry this year and each competitor has a 40% chance of entering and entrants are independent then we could model this situation with the formula

=RISKBinomial(5,.4).

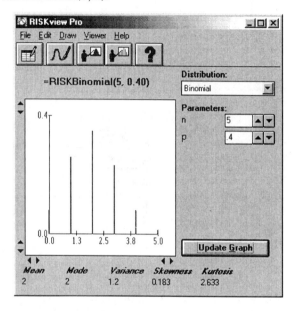

The Normal Random Variable

Used to model a continuous, symmetric (or bell-shaped random variable). The formula

   =RISKNormal(100,15)

will yield

68% of time value between 85 and 115

95% of time value between 70 and 130

99.7% of time value between 55 and 145

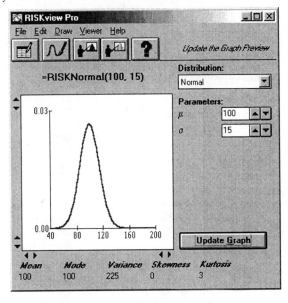

RISKTriang

Enables us to model a nonsymmetrical continuous random variable. Generalizes the well-known idea of best case, worst case and most likely scenario. For example,

=RISKTriang(.2, .4, .8)

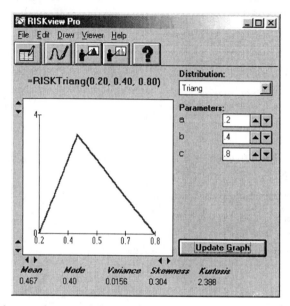

could be used to model market share if we felt worst case market share was 20%, most likely market share was 40% and best case market share was 80%.

Note that probability that market share would be, say, between 30% and 40% would just be area under this "triangle" between .3 and .4. Entire triangle has area = 1. This fact determines the height of the triangle.

RISKTrigen Function

Sometimes we want to use a triangular random variable but we are not sure of the absolute best and worst possibility. We may believe that there is a 10% chance market share will be less than or equal to 30%, most likely share is 40%, and there is a 10% chance that share will exceed 75%. RISKTrigen function is used in this situation. The formula

=RISKTrigen(.3,.4,.75,10,90)

would be appropriate for this situation .Then @RISK draws a triangle which yields

- *10% chance that market share is less than or equal to 30%. This requires a worst possible market share of around 20%.*

- *Most likely market share is 40%.*

- *10% chance that market share is greater than or equal to 75%. This requires a best possible best market share of around 95%.*

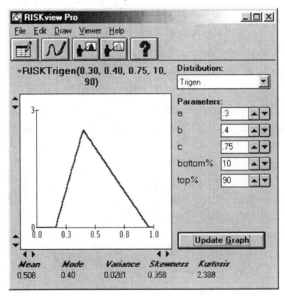

Again, probability of a market share between 20% and 50% is just area under triangle between 20% and 50%.

RISKUniform Function

Suppose a competitor's bid is equally likely to be anywhere between 10 and 30 thousand dollars. This can be modeled by a uniform random variable with the formula

=*RISKUniform(10,30).*

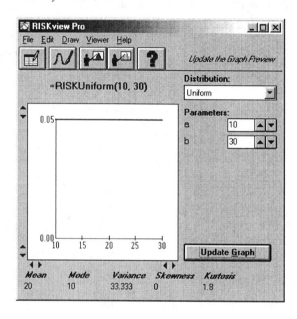

Again, this function makes any bid between 10 and 30 (thousand) dollars equally likely. Probability of a bid between, say 15 and 28 thousand would be area of rectangle bounded by x = 15 and x = 28. This would equal (28 - 15)(.05) = .65.

The RISKGeneral Function

What if a continuous random variable does not appear to follow a normal or triangular distribution? We can model it with the =RISKGeneral function.

Example   Suppose that a market share of between 0 and 60% is possible. A 45% share is most likely. There are five market-share levels for which we feel comfortable about comparing their relative likelihood (see table).

Market Share	Relative Likelihood
10%	1
20%	6
45%	8
50%	7
55%	6

Thus a market share of 45% is 8 times as likely as 10%; 20% and 55% are equally likely, etc. Note this cannot be triangular because then 20% would be (20/45) as likely as peak of 45% and 20% is .75 as likely as 45%.

To model this enter the formula

=RISKGeneral(0,60,{10,20,45,50,55},{1,6,8,7,6}).

The syntax of RISKGeneral is as follows:

1) *Begin with the smallest and largest possible values.*

2) *Then enclose in {} the numbers for which you feel you can compare relative likelihoods.*

3) *Finally enclose in {} the relative likelihoods of the numbers you have previously listed.*

Running this in @RISK yields the following output:

	A	B	C	D	E	F	G
1		EXAMPLE OF					
2		RISKGENERAL					
3		DISTRIBUTION					
4							
5				Minimum	0		
6				Maximum	60		
7				Specified Points			
8				10	1		
9				20	6		
10				45	8		
11				50	7		
12				55	6		
13		45.28889	=RISKGENERAL(0,60,{10,20,45,50,55},{1,6,8,7,6})				

Distribution for DISTRIBUTION

Note 20 is 6/8 as likely as 45; 10 is 1/8 as likely as 45, 50 is 7/8 as likely as 45, 55 is 6/8 as likely as 45, etc. In between the given points, the density function changes at a linear rate. Thus 30 would have a likelihood of

$$6 + \frac{(30-20)*(8-6)}{(45-20)} = 6.8$$

Modeling Correlations

Suppose we have 3 Normal random variables each having mean 0 and standard deviation 1 which are correlated as follows:

Variable 1 and Variable 2 have a .7 correlation.

Variable 1 and Variable 3 have a .8 correlation.

Variable 2 and Variable 3 have a .75 correlation.

To model this correlation structure we use the *=RISKCorrmat* function.

Simply enter your correlation matrix somewhere in worksheet(we chose C27:E29)

	C	D	E	F	G	H	I
27	1	0.7	0.8				
28	0.7	1	0.75				
29	0.8	0.75	1				
30							
31	Variable 1	0	RiskCorrmat($C$27:$E$29,1)+RiskNormal(0,1)				
32	Variable 2	0	RiskCorrmat($C$27:$E$29,2)+RiskNormal(0,1)				
33	Variable 3	0	RiskCorrmat($C$27:$E$29,3)+RiskNormal(0,1)				

For each variable type in front of the variable's actual distribution the syntax

=RiskCorrMat(Matrix, i)+.

Here *Matrix* (C27:E29 in this case) indicates where the correlation matrix resides and i is the column of the correlation matrix which contains the correlations for variable i . Thus for Variable 1 correlations come from first column of correlation matrix.

The + sign is just used to tell @RISK to correlate the riskfunctions after the + sign; it does not indicate addition.

If you run a simulation and extract the data for cells D31:D33 you will find

- Each cell has a mean of around 0 and a standard deviation around 1.
- Each cell follows a normal distribution.
- D31 has around a .7 correlation with D32.
- D31 has around a .8 correlation with D33.
- D32 has around a .75 correlation with D33.

RISKTNormal Function

The =RISKTNormal function is used to model a normal random variable whose value is truncated at a lower and upper value. For example,

=RISKTNormal(10,2,9,11)

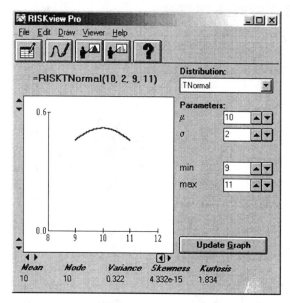

generates a normal random variable with mean 10 and standard deviation 2. If the random variable assumes a value between 9 (The lower truncation value) and 11 (The upper truncation value) that value is retained. Otherwise, another value if generated. The truncation values must be within 5 standard deviations of the mean.

RISKPert Function

The =RISKPert function is similar to the =RISKTriang function. The =RISKPert function is used to model duration of projects. For example,

=RISKPert(5,10,20)

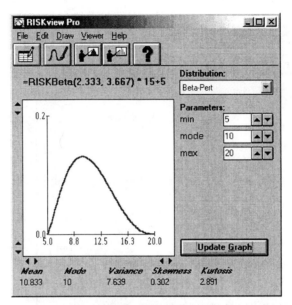

would be used to model the duration of an activity which always takes at least 5 days, never takes more than 20 days, and is most likely to take 10 days. Whie the =RISKTriang has a piecewise linear density function, the =RISKPert density has no linear segments. It is a special case of a Beta random variable.

Index